I love ♣ Ponies

Louise Pritchard

BARRON'S

First edition for the United States and Canada published
in 2007 by Barron's Educational Series, Inc.

First published in 2007 by Oxford University Press
Text copyright © Oxford University Press 2007
Illustrations © Sugar Cubes Publishing 2007

All inquiries should be addressed to:
Barron's Educational Series, Inc.
250 Wireless Boulevard
Hauppauge, New York 11788
www.barronseduc.com

Originated by Oxford University Press
Great Clarendon Street
Oxford, Great Britain OX2 6DP

Created by BOOKWORK Ltd.

ISBN-13: 978-0-7641-3790-7
ISBN-10: 0-7641-3790-5

Library of Congress Control Number: 2006939683

Printed in China

9 8 7 6 5 4 3 2 1

contents

4 Sugar Cubes ponies

horses and ponies
6 the horse family
8 about horses and ponies
10 horse and pony breeds
14 parts of a pony
16 pony colors
18 pony markings
20 how ponies move
22 pony senses
24 pony language
26 living together
28 growing up

looking after a pony
30 handling a pony
32 living in a stable
34 living in a field
36 grooming a pony
38 feeding a pony

pony tack
40 the saddle and bridle
42 putting on a bridle
44 putting on a saddle

riding lessons
46 be prepared
48 first riding lesson
52 moving off

54 working horses and ponies
58 famous horses and ponies

60 glossary
62 addresses and Web sites
64 index

Sugar Cubes ponies

Welcome to the Sugar Cubes Stables Riding School. There are twelve Sugar Cube friends living at the stables. They all appear in this book and they are going to tell you all about horses and ponies.

1 Jacques is a Camargue horse. He was born on February 19th. His star sign is Aquarius. He is patient and friendly, but he can be a bit of a know-it-all.

2 Daisy is a Thoroughbred foal. Her star sign is Leo and she was born on August 11th. She likes attention!

3 Monty is a polo pony but he does not play polo any more. His star sign is Aries and he was born on April 17th. He likes to tell everyone what to do!

4 Coco is a Knabstrup. Her star sign is Gemini and her birthday is June 13th. She used to be a circus pony and is very good at doing tricks.

5 Midnight is an Icelandic horse. Born on May 1st, her star sign is Taurus. She is friendly, practical, and creative, and never loses an argument!

6 Wishes is a Shetland pony. Her birthday is December 31st and her star sign is Capricorn. She is a bit timid, but she can charm anyone.

the ponies

The horses and ponies at the Sugar Cubes Stables are all different **breeds** and have different characters. They are all great friends and love to get together to talk about what they have been doing all day.

They give riding lessons to children nearly every day, all except Daisy, of course, who is still a **foal**. When the children come, the ponies are nearly always friendly and helpful. Some of them, like Sugar Cubes, can be a bit naughty, but they are just having fun.

the ponies say

Look for all of us in this book. We will give you lots of fascinating facts about the world of horses and ponies.

7 Obi is a Welsh Mountain pony. His star sign is Scorpio and his birthday is October 25th. He is reliable and helpful.

8 Pebbles is a Dartmoor pony. Her birthday is March 3rd and her star sign is Pisces. She is a bit shy and nervous.

9 Sugar Cubes is a Welsh pony. He was born on October 15th and his star sign is Libra. He was the first pony at the stables.

10 Indie is an Appaloosa, born on July 22nd. Her star sign is Cancer. She is descended from horses bred 200 years ago by native North Americans.

11 Thistle is a Highland pony. Her star sign is Sagittarius and her birthday is November 29th. She is loving and very friendly.

12 Sinbad is an Arab. He was born on September 19th so his star sign is Virgo. He is fiery and brave but he has a soft heart. He hates mess!

the horse family

Horses and ponies belong to a family of animals called *Equidae*. "Family" is the name we give to animals that are the same sort of shape and live in the same sort of way. Animals in a family are divided into species. Animals of the same species, such as the horse species, all look very similar.

the relatives

Other **species** in the horse's **family** are zebras, the donkey, wild asses of Africa and Asia, and a wild horse called Przewalski's horse. Horses and ponies that live with humans have been **domesticated**. Donkeys have been domesticated too. Other species live in the wild or in zoos.

▶ Zebras live wild in Africa. They are easy to recognize by their black and white stripes.

early horses

Animals in the horse family are descended from an animal called *Hyracotherium*. It lived 54 million years ago and was 14 inches (35 cm) tall. Instead of having one toe protected by a **hoof**, like a horse, it had four hooved toes on its front feet and three on its back feet.

▶ *Hyracotherium* was the size of a small dog. It ate leaves from low bushes.

big and little

Humans have bred horses and donkeys to look different from other animals of the same species. For example, the Mammoth Jack is a very large donkey. The Falabella is a very small horse.

▲ The Mammoth Jack is about 56 inches (142 cm) tall.

▲ The Falabella is only about 28 inches (70 cm) tall.

Indie says

There once was a sort of zebra called a quagga. The last one died in 1883 but scientists are trying to re-create it.

▼ Przewalski's horse is the only species of truly wild horse. A few live wild in Asia. Some live in zoos.

pony fact

❤ The foal of a female horse and a male donkey is called a mule. The foal of a male horse and a female donkey is called a hinny.

about horses and ponies

Horses and ponies are the same species. They are really all horses, and the main difference between them is that ponies are smaller than horses. Ponies can be more mischievous than horses, but this often makes them great fun to ride.

happy pony

A pony should have a lovely shiny coat, bright eyes, and **alert** ears that move to pick up sounds.

A healthy pony will eat up its food well. If it drops lots out of its mouth it could mean there is something wrong with its teeth. A pony should move easily. If it does not, something is hurting it. The veterinarian will find out what is wrong.

pony facts

♥ Horses and ponies usually have 40 teeth.

♥ Horses have an "official" birthday on January 1st or August 1st, depending on where you live.

♥ Horses and ponies can live for 20 or 30 years if they are well looked after.

A healthy pony will take an interest in anything that happens nearby. It may run from something strange at first, but it will come back to investigate.

measuring a pony

A pony's height is measured at the **withers**, the high bit at the bottom of its neck. It can be given in inches or in **hands**. A hand is 4 inches (10 cm). So a pony that is 13.2 hands high is 54 inches (1.37 m) high. It is fun to find out the weight of a pony, too.

◀ You can find a pony's height with a measuring stick. The pony must be standing straight.

▲ It is easy to find a pony's weight with a weightape. It's a bit like measuring your waist.

telling a pony's age

A foal has a set of baby teeth called **milk teeth**. These are gradually replaced by permanent teeth by the age of five. As a pony gets older, its teeth get worn down and change shape. This can help people to tell how old a pony is.

◀ A young pony's teeth are straight and should meet at the front. As a pony gets older, its teeth begin to slope outwards.

Sugar Cubes says

Horses and ponies can go to sleep standing up. They can lock their back legs in position so that they do no fall over.

horse and pony breeds

A breed is a group of horses or ponies that look similar and have the same characteristics. The foal of two members of a breed will be similar to its parents too. There are many different breeds of horses and ponies that have developed over time.

horse breeds

Many breeds developed a long time ago as groups of horses became suited to living in certain places. Then humans began to use horses. They gave them better food and kept the ones they wanted. New breeds of horses developed that could carry loads or run fast.

Coco says

I am a breed of horse called a Knabstrup. This breed comes from Denmark. The horses all have a spotted coat and are intelligent.

The Appaloosa is an American breed known for its spots, but not all horses with spots are Appaloosas. Horses of this breed are athletic, sensible, and willing to work.

Some people think the Arab is the most beautiful breed of all. Its neck is arched and its face is described as "dished." This means its nose is slightly turned up.

The Lipizzaner is famous for being used by the riders of the Spanish Riding School of Vienna. It learns to perform lots of special movements.

pony facts

♥ Most horses are more than 58 inches (1.47 m) or 14.2 hands tall. Most ponies are smaller than this.

♥ Many horses and ponies are a mixture of breeds. They can be called a "type."

♥ Horses that belong to a breed have their names put in a special book called a "stud book."

▲ The Quarterhorse was used by cowboys to herd cattle. Its large quarters give it speed and power.

◄ The Thoroughbred is the fastest breed. Its long back legs help it to gallop fast. Racehorses are Thoroughbreds.

heavy horses

These are large horses that were originally bred to pull heavy loads and vehicles. They are very strong. Most heavy horses are more than 64 inches (1.63 m) tall.

▲ The Clydesdale is the most elegant heavy horse.

▲ The Shire is descended from medieval war horses.

horse and pony breeds

pony breeds

There are several **native** pony breeds. These live naturally in particular places in the world. Many have existed for thousands of years. Some breeds are **hardy** because they come from places where the weather is bad. Other breeds are **sure-footed** because they developed where the ground is stony. As with horses, humans have made their own versions of native breeds, and some new ones too.

▲ The Caspian is the oldest breed. It may have been in ancient Egypt 3,000 years ago.

Obi says

I am a Welsh Mountain pony. Ponies of this breed are very beautiful, like me. They are also brave, tough, kind, and full of life.

▲ The Dartmoor pony first lived on moors in England. A few still live there. Modern ponies are excellent for riding.

▲ The Welsh pony is different than the Welsh Mountain pony, but it is descended from it. It is the perfect riding pony.

▲ The New Forest pony is friendly and sure-footed. Some ponies still live in the New Forest in England.

▲ The Shetland pony is only about 40 inches (101 cm) tall. It comes from the rocky, windy islands north of Scotland.

▲ The Fjord pony comes from Norway. It is descended from Przewalski's horse. It is strong, brave, and tough.

▼ The Connemara pony is a brilliant jumper. It is fast and sensible and possibly the best pony to ride in a competition. The breed comes from Ireland.

ponies that are horses!

Some breeds of horse are the size of ponies but are called horses. The Camargue from France and the Icelandic horse are both under 58 inches (1.47 m) tall.

▲ Camargue horses still live wild in France.

▲ Icelandic horses can carry adults a long way.

parts of a pony

Ponies are built to move easily. To survive in the wild, they must move around to find food and water and quickly run from danger. Humans can help domesticated ponies that have a problem, but it is best for a pony when everything works properly.

▼ These are the main points of the horse. They are the same for horses and ponies.

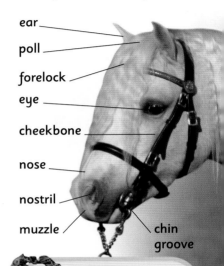

ear
poll
forelock
eye
cheekbone
nose
nostril
muzzle
chin groove

points of the horse

All of the parts of horses and ponies have special names. The names are called the **points of the horse**. It is useful to know all the different names because people use these when they describe a pony. If you have lessons at a riding school, your instructor will use the names too. Knowing the points of the horse will help you understand what you are being told. The left side of a pony is called the **near side**. The right side is called the **off side**. You will usually get on a pony and lead it from the near side.

Jacques says
The shape of a pony is called its conformation. This includes things like how long its back is, what shape its neck is, and whether its feet turn in. A pony with good conformation is able to move and bend better.

skeleton

The skeleton gives a pony its shape and supports its body. It also protects **organs** in the body, such as the heart and the liver.

parts of the foot

The **frog** is a v-shaped pad under the foot. It grips the ground as the pony walks and acts like a cushion. The **wall** is the outside of the hoof. It grows like your fingernails. It does not hurt a pony to have a shoe nailed on as long as the nails do not touch the **white line**.

frog
bar
sole
white line
wall

▲ The underside of a pony's foot

mane
crest
withers
back
loins
croup
dock

shoulder
elbow
belly
flank
stifle

knee
hock joint

cannon bone

tendons

coronet
tail

pastern
fetlock joint
hoof
heel

15

pony colors

The first thing you will notice about a pony is probably the color of its coat. Color is an important part of the description of a pony. Ponies of some breeds are accepted as a member of the breed only if they are the right color. Some colors are more common than others. A black pony is rare. Gray and bay ponies are the most common.

▼ A white pony is called gray. It has black skin and a mixture of white and black hairs in its coat.

▲ A dappled gray pony has patches of pale and darker gray.

coat colors

Horses and ponies come in different colors. There are also different shades and variations of a color. For example, gray ponies vary from white to dark gray. A gray pony can be **fleabitten** (white with dark specks), **dappled** (with circular patches of paler gray) or **iron** gray (dark gray). A **bay** pony is a reddish color but it can be light, bright, or dark bay. A **chestnut** pony is ginger colored but it can be light, dark or liver chestnut, which is the darkest.

▲ bay—reddish with black points

▲ palomino—gold with a white mane and tail

what color is it?

A pony's color includes its tail, mane, muzzle, the tips of its ears, and the ends of its legs. These are called the **points**. A bay pony has black points. Chestnut and black ponies are the same all over, except for white markings. A **paint** or **pinto** has large black and white patches (**piebald**), or patches of white and any color but black (**skewbald**). A **strawberry roan** has a mixture of chestnut and white hairs.

▲ chestnut

▲ black

▲ piebald/paint

▲ strawberry roan

pony markings

Lots of ponies have white patches on their face and legs. Some have other markings on their body, such as a "whorl" of hair or a "flesh mark" where their skin shows through. It will help you to recognize a pony if you know what markings it has.

▶ When a pony has a white stocking or white sock, it usually has a white hoof to go with it.

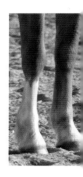

white markings

Purebred horses and ponies are usually **registered**. Any markings they have are described in their registration papers. The best way to describe a marking is to say what part of the body it covers. But there are names for many markings that people often use. For example, white up to the knee or hock is called a **stocking**. White up to the fetlock is a **sock**. A white mark on the forehead is a **star**. A narrow white mark down the face is a **stripe**, and a white mark between the nostrils is called a **snip**.

dorsal stripe

Some dark-skinned ponies have a stripe along the back. This is called a **dorsal stripe**. These ponies may also have stripy markings on their legs, called **zebra markings**. Early horses had these markings. They may have helped to hide the horses from their enemies.

▼ dorsal stripe

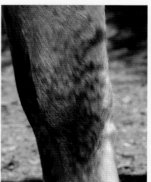
▲ zebra markings

▼ A pony of any color can have a white marking on its face. Some ponies have a white face, where the white goes right across the nose and over the eyes.

◀ stripe and snip

▲ star

▲ white face

▶ blaze and white forehead

how ponies move

The ways in which a pony moves along are called paces, or gaits. Ponies have four main gaits. They are walk, trot, canter and gallop. The pony's steps are different for each gait. One complete set of steps in a gait is called a stride.

▼ If you listen carefully when a pony walks, you will hear the four beats as it puts its feet on the ground.

pony fact
❤ If a pony is limping, we say it is lame. The vet will watch the pony trot up and down to determine which foot or leg is hurting.

walk

This is the slowest **gait**. It is called a **four-beat** gait because the pony moves its four feet one at a time. It moves a back foot, then the front foot on the same side, then the other back and front feet.

trot

When a pony trots, it moves its front and back feet together in diagonal pairs. So trotting is a **two-beat** gait. It is faster than the walk.

◀ In trot, the pony springs from two feet on to the other two feet.

canter

The canter is faster than the trot. It is a **three-beat** gait. The pony moves one back foot, then the other back foot and opposite front foot together, then the other front foot on its own. This front leg is called the **leading leg**.

▶ When a pony canters, it looks a bit like it is skipping.

special gaits

Some horses and ponies have extra gaits. Icelandic horses can **tolt**. This is a natural four-beat gait a bit like a running walk. American Saddlebreds and Racking horses are popular for a special gait called the **rack** that is comfortable to ride and flashy in the show ring.

gallop

At the gallop, ponies move their feet in the same order as in the canter. But the four feet touch the ground separately, making it a **four-beat** gait. This is the fastest gait. Racehorses can gallop at about 43 mph (70 km/h).

Midnight says

In the wild, horses and ponies do not move fast unless they have to run away from danger. They usually walk or trot, and not for more than ten minutes.

▲ A galloping horse moves its legs fast. It takes all four feet off the ground at the same time before starting the step sequence again.

pony senses

Ponies have extremely good senses of touch, sight, smell, taste, and hearing. These senses are important because ponies use them all the time. They use them to find out about new things, recognize friends, and know quickly when an enemy is nearby, which gives them time to escape.

five senses

You may think ponies have a "sixth sense" because they notice things that you don't. But it's probably just their five senses working better than yours. In the wild especially, horses and ponies use their senses to help them survive. They look, listen, and smell for danger. And they use taste and smell to check their food.

new smell

When a pony makes this face, it is called **flehmen**. It may do this if it smells something unusual. It may help it to recognize the smell next time.

1 Touch—ponies are sensitive all over. They touch as a way of talking, which is why friends groom each other.

Sinbad says

Horses and ponies have sensitive whiskers around their nose and their eyes. They use these for sensing nearby objects.

2 Hearing—ponies can hear sounds several miles away. They pick up sounds coming from any direction.

3 Sight—a pony's eyes are set on the side of its head so it can see nearly all around its body. There is a small area directly behind it that it cannot see.

4 Smell—this is an important sense for a pony. Ponies can recognize a friend by smell, find their way home by smell, and can find water by smell.

5 Taste—ponies like salty and sweet things. They can tell if food is good or bad, but have to learn what tastes nice.

pony language

Ponies use their bodies to show each other what they are thinking. They will use the same body language with you. They will also watch your body language to try to determine what you are thinking.

Ears forward—alert and happy

Ears back—cross or frightened

One ear to the side—listening

▲ If you watch a pony's ears you will see them move backward and forward to pick up sounds. The ears will also show you what mood a pony is in.

talking

Talk to a pony when you are with it. It will know from the tone of your voice that you are a friend. But ponies cannot learn your language so it is up to you to try to learn some pony language. When you get to know a pony well, you will begin to recognize its body language.

◀ If you watch a pony carefully you will learn what it is thinking.

pony moods

Ponies have bad days and good days, just like you! Sometimes a pony may not want a fuss. It may lift a back leg to say "I am warning you. I may kick you if you go on doing that." If it is angry it may try to bite. Don't let a pony kick you or bite you. Tell it off, but do not be rough. If a pony nudges you with its nose, it probably wants attention. If it **paws** the ground or stamps, it is impatient—maybe for its food!

▼ This pony is showing off. It is holding its head and tail high and lifting up its feet.

pony fact
❤ Ponies don't have conversations with their friends like you do. They just need to tell each other what they are feeling. Then they can avoid any violent arguments.

Thistle and Monty say
Ponies sometimes whinny, or neigh, to call to their friends. Some ponies have learned to attract the attention of their owners by whinnying.

living together

In the wild, horses and ponies live in family groups called herds. A herd will contain males and females and horses or ponies of all ages. Domesticated ponies prefer to live with other ponies too. If there is only one pony, it may like cows or sheep for company.

the herd

In a **herd**, there is always a boss. Under the boss, each pony has a position in the herd. They all know who can tell who what to do. This stops arguments.

Sometimes one pony will **challenge** another to try to get a higher position. It is the same with a group of ponies in a field. When a new pony is introduced to a group, it has to sort out what its position is.

The leader of a group will round up the others to remind them who is boss. The ponies must do what the boss says.

► Often, there will be close friends in a group who stay close together. These friends are mustangs. They live in a wild herd in North America.

▼ Chincoteague ponies live on an island off the east coast of Virginia. Every year the herd is rounded up. The ponies swim to the mainland where some are sold.

Jacques says

A pony will treat you as a member of its herd. When it meets you it will determine who is boss. You must make sure that it knows that you are boss. Be firm but kind. Then it will try to do what you say.

► Young horses and ponies learn by playing. They will often play at fighting. This is practice for when they grow up and have to find their position in the herd. They do not hurt each other.

growing up

A female horse or pony is called a mare. Mares usually give birth to one baby at a time. Twins are rare. A baby horse or pony is called a foal. Most foals are born in the spring when there is lots of fresh grass to eat and the weather is not too cold.

young foals

A **foal** is born with a furry coat to keep it warm and a short fluffy tail. It will lose this coat after about two months. It has very long legs compared to its body. It needs these to keep up with its mother. A foal may not have teeth, but its baby teeth will soon appear.

▲ A new foal will be able to stand within half an hour of being born. Very soon, it will be able to run beside its mother.

Daisy says

At six months old, I am able to live away from my mother because I have people to look after me. In the wild, young ponies leave their mother when they are a few years old to start their own herds.

mother and baby

A **mare** will look after her foal very carefully, protecting it from any danger. In the wild, all the adult ponies help to look after the foals. They take turns eating and sleeping. There is always at least one pony watching over the foals. It warns the rest of the herd of any danger.

▲ As they grow up, foals learn from their mother. For example, they learn what is dangerous and what is safe.

◀ A foal drinks milk from its mother right after it is born. After a few weeks it will begin to eat grass too. Before it grows up a bit, it is difficult for a foal to reach the grass because its legs are too long!

handling a pony

When you are with a pony, you must handle it properly—for your safety and for the pony's safety. Most ponies do not want to hurt anyone. They just behave as they would in the wild and want to protect themselves from possible danger.

Pebbles says

Always be calm and quiet around ponies. Then they will be calm and quiet too. But do not go up to a pony without letting it know you are there. You may give it a fright and it may kick.

catching a pony

A **halter** is the best thing to use to catch, lead, and tie up a pony. You may need some help to catch a pony because some do not want to be caught and are naughty. Walk toward the pony from the front and at a slight angle so that it can see you. Talk to it all the time and hold out your hand so that it can smell you too. Show it that you are not nervous.

Hold the carrot in the palm of your hand. Keep your hand flat.

▶ Hold out your hand to the pony firmly. Let the pony take the carrot gently from your hand.

giving treats

When your pony has been good, you may like to give it a treat, such as a carrot or an apple. Keep your hand as flat as you can. Hold your fingers and thumb together so that the pony does not bite one by mistake.

▼ First put the rope of the halter over the pony's neck. Then use both hands to put the noseband over the pony's nose.

▲ Then you can pass the long strap over the pony's poll and do up the buckle.

▲ Hold the lead rope with one hand near the pony's chin and one hand near the end.

tying up a pony

Always tie up a pony to a loop of string. If the pony panics, the string will break and the pony will not hurt itself. Use a **quick-release knot**, which you can undo quickly in an emergency.

This end goes to the pony's halter.

1

3

2

Pull this end to undo the knot.

◄▲ Follow these pictures to tie a quick-release knot. Ask someone to help you.

This is the loose end.

It is useful to have a stable in which to put a pony. You can handle it more easily in a stable than in a field and you can look after it if it is ill. A stable also keeps a pony warm and dry in the winter and protects it from heat, flies, and hot sun in the summer.

a stable life

Living in a stable is very different from living in the wild. A pony's owner must provide everything it needs. As well as food and water, a pony must have daily exercise and company so that it does not get bored and unhappy. All ponies like to spend some time in a field.

▲ Good friends can share a stable for some of the time if there is enough room for two.

the pony's bed

Ponies like to lie down in their stable sometimes and they need to have comfortable **bedding** to lie on. Most ponies have a bed of **straw** or wood **shavings**, and some have torn-up paper. Sometimes a stable has **rubber matting** to keep the floor dry. Any dirty bedding must be removed every day. This is called **mucking out**.

▲ This is what you use for mucking out.

▲ Shavings are easy to take out with a shavings fork.

the stable

A stable must be safe and comfortable for the pony with plenty of fresh air. A pony is often fed on the floor of the stall or in a **manger** fixed to the wall in one corner.

Sinbad says

When you go into or leave a pony's stable, remember to shut the door carefully so that the pony cannot get out. This could cause a bad accident.

▲ Ponies like to see what is going on around them in the stable yard.

▲ Straw is comfortable but it is too dusty for some ponies.

▲ Rubber matting is best with some bedding on top.

pony facts

❤ A pony's stall must be about 12 feet x 10 feet (3.6 m x 3 m) or bigger so it has plenty of room to move around and lie down or roll.

❤ A pony's halter should be taken off when it is left untied in its stall.

living in a field

Ponies like it best if they can spend at least part of every day in a field with their friends. Then they can graze, stretch their legs, and do what they want. This is what they would do in the wild.

spring and summer

In spring, new grass begins to grow, which ponies love. A good field may have some dandelions and clover growing in it too. But the ponies must not eat too much rich grass because it will make them fat and even ill. In the summer, there are flies and biting insects. Some ponies wear a thin rug and even a net over their eyes to keep off the flies.

▼ Ponies love to roll. They may do this to rub their back or dry off their coat. Then they get up and have a good shake.

drinking water

All ponies must have clean water in their field to drink. Many fields have a **trough** with its own water supply. The water must be checked every day. In summer the ponies may drink it all. In winter it may freeze.

Midnight says

Ponies swish off annoying flies with their tail. They may stand head to tail with a friend so that they can keep the flies off each other's face.

▼ In the winter, there is not much grass to eat so ponies may need extra hay.

autumn and winter

A healthy pony will be very happy living in a field all year round if it is warm enough and has enough to eat and drink. In autumn and winter, ponies grow a thick coat. This keeps them warm, even when it snows. Ponies that do not have a thick coat wear a rug in the winter. This helps to keep them clean as well as warm and dry.

grooming a pony

When you brush a pony, it is called grooming. You groom a pony to get out the dirt from its coat and make it tidy. Grooming is also good for the pony's muscles. Most ponies enjoy being groomed.

▼ Use a hoof pick to pick out a pony's feet. Always use it from the heel toward the toe.

▲ Brush the mane with a body brush. Do a little bit at a time. Don't forget the forelock. Try to make the pony's mane lie on the off side of the neck.

the kit

Use a **body brush** for most grooming and clean it with a **metal curry comb**. Use a **dandy brush** or **rubber curry comb** for muddy bits on the pony. Use sponges to wipe the eyes, nose, and dock.

rubber curry comb

sponge

dandy brush

metal curry comb

body brush

hoof pick

grooming

Start by picking out mud and stones from the pony's feet. Then do the mane, the tail, and the whole body. It is hard work to **groom** a pony properly. If a pony lives in a field without a blanket, you should not bathe it. It needs the oil in its coat to keep it warm. Just get off the mud with a dandy brush.

Wishes says

Use a body brush to brush a pony's tail. Do a little bit at a time and be careful not to pull the hairs. Use your fingers to undo any tangles.

picking up a foot

A pony should pick up its feet when it is asked. The **farrier** will need to do its shoes. The vet may need to look at its feet if it is lame. And you will need to lift its feet to pick them out. Stand close to the pony's leg, facing the back of the pony. Bend over or squat to look at the feet. Never sit on the ground near a pony.

1

2

▲ Run your nearest hand down the pony's leg to the fetlock joint.

▲ Say "up" and the pony should lift its foot. Rest it in your hand.

▶ Brush the face gently with a body brush. Be careful around the pony's eyes.

▼ Use the body brush to brush a pony's body. After a few strokes, scrape the brush across the metal curry comb to remove the dirt.

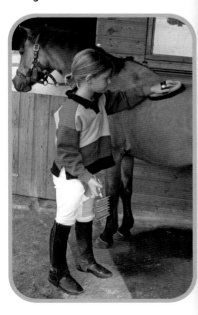

feeding a pony

The natural food of horses and ponies in the wild is grass. They eat a little bit at a time so that they never get too full. We must try to feed domestic ponies in the same way as they would eat in the wild.

◄ Ponies love grass. They will move around the field to find the bits they like best.

▲ Carrots are healthy treats. They must be cut lengthwise because round pieces can get stuck in a pony's throat.

food types

Ponies that live in a field eat grass. They may need some **hay** (dried grass) in the winter when there is not so much grass to eat. Ponies that live in a stable eat hay. If a pony is ridden a lot and works hard, it may need food such as **oats** or **grain**. These will give it the extra energy it needs. A pony must not be given too much to eat because this will make it fat and often ill. Even grass can be fattening.

pellet feed

mix of grains

Sugar Cubes says

It is important that ponies have clean, fresh water available to drink at all times. They need to drink about 6.5 gallons (30 litres) of water every day to make the systems in their bodies work properly.

▲ Horse feeds contain all the vitamins and minerals a pony needs. But a pony must eat mostly grass or hay.

feeding hay

Some people feed hay loose on the ground, which is the most natural place for the pony. But the pony may tread on it and make it dirty. Then it will be no good to eat and will be wasted. At a horse show, one way to feed hay is in a **haynet**. The haynet is hung up where the pony can reach it easily. It should be hung through a ring on the stable wall or trailer.

1

▶ To fill a haynet, loosen the string and open the net wide. Push in the hay. Be careful not to push in the string too!

2

▲ When you have pushed in enough hay, pull the string to close the net. Then it is ready to be tied to a ring using a quick-release knot.

pony fact

❤ Some plants are poisonous to ponies and can kill them. Ragwort is a yellow flower that grows in some places and is very poisonous.

the saddle and bridle

When a pony is ridden it wears a saddle and bridle. These are called the pony's tack. Most saddles and bridles are made of leather. They will last a long time if they are looked after properly.

the saddle

A **saddle** goes on the pony's back. It stops the pony's spine digging into the rider. It also makes it easier for the pony to carry the rider. But it must fit the pony properly so that it does not rub it or hurt it. The saddle has a **girth** to keep it on the pony. The girth goes under the pony's tummy. The rider's feet go in **stirrup irons**, which are attached to the saddle by **stirrup leathers**.

▼ The parts of a saddle have special names.

▼ Tack must be cleaned regularly with water and saddle soap.

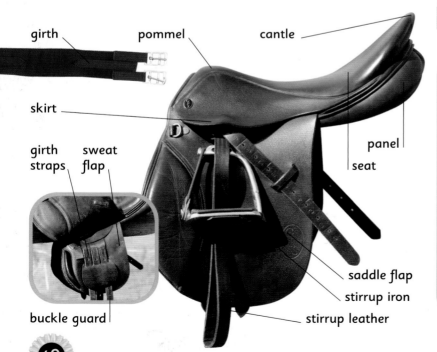

girth

pommel

cantle

skirt

girth straps

sweat flap

panel

seat

buckle guard

saddle flap

stirrup iron

stirrup leather

pony facts

❤ Most saddles are built around a frame called a tree.

❤ There are many types of saddle and bridle. They are used for different types of riding, such as dressage or jumping.

western tack

Lots of people like riding in the western style. This is the way cowboys in the Old West rode. The horses and ponies wear special tack. Cowboys spent a long time on their horses, so western tack is comfortable. It is designed to make it easy for cowboys to do their work.

▲ Today, western tack is often decorated with shiny pieces of metal. The leather often has patterns carved into it.

▼ The parts of a bridle have special names, like a saddle.

browband

cheekpiece

noseband

headpiece

the bridle

A rider uses a **bridle** to control the pony's head. The **reins** are used to help steer the pony. They are attached to a **bit** in the pony's mouth. A bridle must fit properly so that it is comfortable for the pony and the bit does not hurt its mouth.

throatlash

keeper

runner

snaffle bit

bit

rein

putting on a bridle

Putting on a bridle may look difficult, but you will soon get the hang of it. Most ponies will keep still while you put on a bridle. Always move quietly and slowly so that you do not frighten the pony. Be gentle and be careful not to bang its teeth with the bit.

Pebbles says

To take off a bridle, undo the noseband and throatlatch. Then bring the bridle over the pony's ears. Don't pull out the bit. Let the pony drop the bit in its own time.

how to put on a bridle

Make sure the pony is tied up properly before you start to put on its bridle. Put on the bridle from the near side. Check that the bridle is straight and all the straps are lying flat before you do up the buckles. When you have done up the buckles, remember to thread the straps through the keepers and runners. This makes the bridle look tidy and stops the straps from coming undone.

▼ Put the reins over the pony's head before you take off the halter. Then you can hold the pony if it tries to walk off.

1

2

▲ Hold the bridle in your right hand. Ask the pony to take the bit by putting your left thumb between its lips where there are no teeth.

check the fit

It is easy to check which hole to use when you do up the buckle on the throatlatch and noseband. The throatlatch should be quite loose or it could stop the pony from breathing easily. This pony has on a simple noseband. It should be loose enough to let the pony open its mouth slightly.

▲ Fit four fingers between the throatlatch and the cheek.

▲ Fit two fingers between the noseband and the face.

pony facts

♥ Bridles come in several different sizes to fit different horses and ponies.

♥ When a pony has its saddle and bridle on and is ready to be ridden we say that it is "tacked up."

3

▲ Put the headpiece over the ears. Then do up the throatlatch.

▶ Do up the noseband. This simple noseband goes above the bit, under the cheekpieces.

4

Tie up the pony while you put on its saddle. Make sure the pony is clean where the saddle and girth go. Mud here would rub the pony and make it sore. You can put on a saddle and numnah together, or you can put on the numnah first.

how to put on a saddle

A pony's saddle can be heavy so you may need help to lift it onto the pony. First check that the numnah is lying flat and the girth is not caught up. Lie the girth across the saddle. Pick up the saddle with the pommel in your left hand and the cantle in your right hand. Be careful not to drop it because this could cause damage. Do not put the saddle down hard on the pony's back. This will frighten the pony and could hurt its back.

▲ Put the saddle and numnah forward on the pony's withers. Then slide them back together.

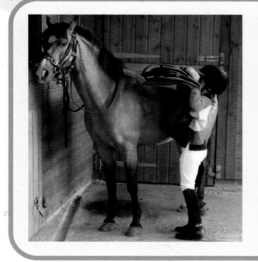

taking off a saddle

Before you take off a saddle, you must **run up the stirrups**. Push the irons to the top of the stirrup leathers and tuck the loop of the leathers through the irons. Then undo the girth on one side and cross it over the saddle. Take off the saddle, pulling it slowly toward you from the near side. Put the saddle away in the **tack room**. Do not put it down on the floor where the pony could tread on it.

▼ Go to the off side of the pony and take down the girth. Make sure it is lying flat. Then, from the near side, bring the girth under the pony's tummy.

▶ Pass the girth under the loop on the numnah if there is one. Buckle the girth to the straps on the saddle.

3

2

Jacques says

When you first do up the girth, a pony may blow out its tummy. Later, it will relax and the girth will be loose. So you must tighten the girth before you get on the pony.

be prepared

When you go riding, the most important thing is to be as safe as possible. Ponies are strong and do not always do what you expect. Accidents can happen, so always do what your teacher, or instructor, tells you.

hard ha
with a
silk

Sinbad says

If you want to learn to ride, it is best to go to a riding school. Your teacher will give you a pony to ride that is just right for you. You will learn to ride correctly, and this will give you lots of confidence.

clothing

You do not have to look smart to ride, but you must wear clothes that are comfortable and safe for riding. Gloves stop the reins from rubbing your hands. It is important that you wear a **hard hat** that fits you, made especially for riding, to protect your head during falls.

▶ Stretchy jodhpurs and short riding boots with a heel are best to ride in.

▲ Some people wear half-chaps around their legs to protect them.

gloves

jodhpurs

riding boots

▼ A body protector is hard and will protect your body if you fall off. The shop assistant will make sure you get one that fits you.

hard velvet-covered hat

body protector

western gear

For western riding, people wear slightly different clothes. Most people wear long jeans and tough boots called **roper boots**. Many riders wear a western hat with a wide brim. But it is best to wear a hard hat, in case you fall off.

hard hat

▲ It is fun to wear your own style of clothes. But always put safety first and wear a hard hat.

first riding lesson

Your first riding lesson will be exciting. You may be a bit nervous, but you will have a quiet pony to ride. Do not worry if you find anything difficult. Your instructor will help you until you get the hang of it.

Obi says

You may be able to stand on a mounting block to get on a pony. This makes it easier to reach the stirrup iron. A mounting block might be a block of wood or stone, or some low steps.

getting on

Getting on a pony is called **mounting**. You usually mount a pony from the near side. The pony must stand still while you mount and not walk off until you are ready. Someone will hold the pony when you are learning. She will hold onto the stirrup on the off side so you do not pull the saddle toward you.

1

▲ Hold the reins in your left hand on the pony's withers. Face the pony's tail and put your left foot in the stirrup.

2

▲ Put your right hand on the far side of the saddle. Spring up to stand in the stirrup. Do not pull on the saddle.

3

▲ Swing your right leg over the pony's back, being careful not to kick it. Put your right foot in the stirrup.

stirrup length

Alter your stirrups when you are on a pony. Put the buckle in a new hole on the leather, then pull the leather to move the buckle to the top. Ask someone to hold the pony if you need two hands at first.

pony fact

♥ Your instructor, or another adult, should always be around to watch when you ride, in case of an accident.

checking the girth

Once you are on the pony you must make sure the girth is tight enough. If it is too loose the saddle could slip around while you are riding. Your instructor will help you tighten the girth. You should check it again later, in case your pony was breathing out the first time.

▶ Put your leg forward and hold up the saddle flap so that your instructor can reach the buckles to tighten the girth.

49

first riding lesson

sitting in the saddle

Sit in the lowest part of the saddle, as straight and tall as you can. Look straight ahead. Hold the reins in front of the saddle. Imagine there is a straight line from the pony's mouth, through your hands to your elbows. Imagine another line going straight down from your shoulder through your hip to your heel.

▶ Rest the balls of your feet on the stirrup irons. Push your heels down and point your toes forward.

◀ Hold one rein in each hand and make a loose fist with your thumb on top. The rein should go between your little and third fingers.

Wishes says

If you sit properly in the saddle it will be easier for you to give the pony clear instructions. It will also make it easier for the pony to understand what you are asking it to do.

getting off

At the end of your lesson you will need to get off the pony! This is called **dismounting**. You usually dismount on the near side. It is best to dismount by taking both feet out of the stirrups at the same time. That way, if the pony spooks while you are getting off, your left foot won't get caught in the stirrup.

▶ Take your feet out of the stirrups. Lean forward and swing your right leg over the pony's back.

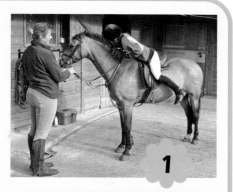

1

▶ Slide down to the ground slowly, keeping hold of the reins in your left hand.

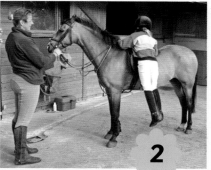

2

3

▶ Bend your knees as you land on the ground. Straighten up quickly so that you are ready to control the pony.

Land as close to the pony as you can.

moving off

During your first lesson, you will learn how to ask a pony to move forward and stop. Later you will learn to trot and canter. Your instructor will teach you how to give signals called aids to the pony.

▼ Use your legs to keep the pony walking forward. If your pony is a bit lazy, you may need to give it a small kick with your heels.

walking and stopping

You ask a pony to walk by squeezing it gently with your legs. If it does not move forward right away, you can give it a nudge with your heels. To stop, you must sit up straight and deep in the saddle. Squeeze the reins and give a firm pull, but not a sharp tug.

trotting

The trot is a bouncy pace. You will learn to go up and down in the saddle in time to the pony's movement. This makes it more comfortable and is called **rising trot**. You will learn **sitting trot**, too, when you sit down all the time.

Sugar Cubes says

To turn left, squeeze the left rein gently and press your right leg against the pony's side, just behind the girth. Do the opposite to turn right. Turn to look where you are going.

▼ Ask the pony to trot by squeezing with your legs. When you want to walk, sit down and pull gently on the reins.

cantering

When you have had several lessons and you can control a pony well at walk and trot, you will learn to canter. This is faster than trot. Do not use the reins to help you stay on. The pony may have a strap around its neck for you to hold onto, or you can hold a bit of mane.

▲ You will learn how to keep your bottom in the saddle when you are cantering. You might find this difficult at first. Some ponies have a more bumpy canter than others.

being led

To begin with, someone may lead the pony for you while you get used to the movement. Or, your instructor may stand in the middle of the riding ring and have the pony circle around her on a long lead rope, called a **lunge line**, while you ride. This helps you learn to balance.

working horses and ponies

Horses and ponies do lots of different work for us. Some horses help people to do their jobs, such as farming, racing, or being in the police force. Other horses help people to have fun just riding or competing.

▼ Thoroughbred horses are used for racing because they can gallop fast. Riders called jockeys ask their horses to race each other. Sometimes they go over jumps.

horses in sport

Many people have horses that are trained to go **racing**. Some people do **show jumping**. They ride a horse over a course of jumps and try not to knock one down. Other riders do **dressage**, when they ask their horses to do special movements. Many horses and ponies enter **show classes**, in which the best-looking one wins.

pony fact
❤ Before cars were invented, horses pulled people in carriages. Today we still use the word "horsepower" to describe the power of an engine.

Monty says
It is fun to go with a pony to a gymkhana. Here you can take part in many different races, such as a sack race, a bending race between poles, or an egg-and-spoon race. Most ponies enjoy the races.

This Australian pony is pulling a carriage in a driving class at a show. The pony and driver look very smart.

working horses and ponies

heavy horses

Some people still use large, strong horses for **plowing** or pulling heavy loads. The horses cannot do the job as quickly as a tractor or a truck, but they do not **pollute** the air with fumes. The horses wear a collar and a **harness** attached to the plow or cart.

▶ Farmers can use Shire horses for plowing.

police horses

Many countries use horses in the police force. The horses are specially chosen for their quiet behavior. Then they are trained so that they are not frightened by things that they might meet in their work, such as traffic, loud noises, or large crowds.

▲ These police horses are on patrol in Florida. They must be well behaved so that their riders can do their job.

◀ It is fun to go for a ride in the countryside. But some horses and ponies get a bit excited when they go out for a casual ride. They want to go fast!

riding horses

The job that most horses and ponies do is letting people enjoy themselves by just riding. The horses enjoy it too. They take their riders through beautiful countryside, along the beach, or even over mountains. People go on riding vacations all over the world, when they can ride different types of horses and see different countries.

pony fact

❤ Horses and ponies have been working for people for about 6,000 years. Ancient tribes first used horses to carry things. Then they began to ride them. It was easier and faster than walking.

famous horses and ponies

▲ Pegasus is a winged horse in a story from ancient Greece. He was ridden by Bellerophon. Pegasus threw off Bellerophon, who fell to his death. Pegasus later flew up to the sky and became a constellation of stars.

People love horses and ponies. They are beautiful animals with personalities. Many stories are written about horses. Some are true and others are make-believe. These horses became famous all over the world.

Thistle says

Trigger is my hero. He starred with his master, American film star Roy Rogers (1911–1998), in many films and on TV. He won an award for one film and had his own fan club. He died in 1965.

horses in stories

Many famous horses and ponies are not real. They are characters in well-known stories. Some of these stories were first told thousands of years ago in **myths** and **legends**. Many others were written in modern times.

► The Trojan horse was a wooden statue in an ancient legend. Greek soldiers hid in the horse to trick the Trojans in a war. The Trojans took the horse into their city. Then the Greeks jumped out and won the battle.

▶ This is Florian, an Andalusian horse. He starred in the films of *The Lord of the Rings.* In the original book by J. R. R. Tolkien (1892–1973), there are many horses. Shadowfax was a gray horse that the wizard Gandalf rode.

pony facts

❤ A horse named Figure founded the Morgan breed, named for Figure's owner Justin Morgan. Marguerite Henry told the story in a book.

❤ Bucephalus was a black horse that helped Alexander the Great (356–323 BCE) create an empire in Asia. They went into many battles together, and when Bucephalus died in battle, Alexander gave him a proper funeral.

❤ Barbaro won many races in America, including the Kentucky Derby. Everybody loved him, but in 2006 he broke his leg during a race. He had long surgery to mend the leg, but despite efforts he could not be saved.

glossary

The world of horses and ponies is full of words that you may not have heard before. Here are some of the words used in this book. The words have an explanation with them to tell you what they mean.

aids The ways in which a rider asks a horse or pony to do something. The legs, hands, body, seat, and voice are aids.

▼ Western riders use a special saddle and bridle.

bit An item that goes in a pony's mouth to help you control it. It is attached to the *reins*.

body language The way in which horses and ponies, and other animals, use their bodies to show others what they are thinking and feeling.

breed A type of horse or pony. All members of a breed are similar.

bridle A piece of *tack* that goes on a horse or pony's head.

canter A three-beat *gait*. It is faster than *trot* and slower than *gallop*.

colt A young male horse or pony up to 4 years old.

conformation The way a horse or pony is put together, which gives it a particular shape. A pony with bad conformation may find it difficult to do certain things.

dismount To get off a horse or pony.

domesticated Horses and ponies that live with humans are described as domesticated.

farrier A person who shoes horses and ponies and looks after their feet.

filly A young female horse or pony up to 4 years old.

foal A baby horse or pony, up to 1 year old.

gait A way in which a horse or pony moves, also called a pace. There are four main gaits.

gallop A four-beat *gait*. It is the fastest gait.

graze To eat grass and other plants growing low on the ground.

groom To brush a horse or pony to clean its coat and make it look tidy.

halter A piece of equipment that goes on a horse or pony's head for leading it or tying it up.

hand A unit of measurement that is often used to measure the height of a horse or pony. One hand is about 4 inches (10 cm).

hay Dried grass, given to horses and ponies to eat.

herd A group of wild horses or ponies.

lame A horse or pony that is limping is described as lame.

lunge line A rope that attaches to the halter with a snap, used to lead the pony.

mount To get on a horse or pony.

points of the horse The names of the different parts of a horse or pony.

reins Two long pieces of bridle attached to the *bit*. The reins are used by a rider to help steer a horse or pony.

saddle A piece of *tack* that goes on a horse or pony's back for the rider to sit in.

senses Horses and ponies use their senses to find out about things around them. The senses are taste, sight, hearing, touch, and smell.

species A type of living thing. Horses and ponies are a species of animal.

straw Dried stalks of wheat, barley, or oats, used for bedding in a stable.

stride When a horse or pony has moved all four feet once at a certain *gait*, it has taken one stride.

tack The equipment used for riding a horse or pony.

trot A two-beat *gait*. It is faster than *walk* and slower than *canter*.

vet A doctor for animals. The word "vet" is short for "veterinarian."

walk A four-beat *gait*. It is the slowest gait.

western riding A way of riding that was started by cowboys in the American West.

61

addresses and web sites

Here is a list of addresses and Web sites where you can find out more about horses and ponies. If you want to learn to ride, start by going to the Pony Club or the American Riding Instructors Association to find an approved riding school.

United States Pony Clubs, Inc.
4041 Iron Works Pike
Lexington, KY 40511
tel: (859) 254-7669
Web site:
www.ponyclub.org

The Pony club is for young people under the age of 25 who are interested in learning to ride and care for ponies. You do not have to have your own pony to belong. Some events and competitions are arranged at riding schools. You can find a club in your area from the Web site.

American Quarter Horse Association
P.O. Box 200
Amarillo, TX 79168
Web site: www.aqha.com

The registering association for American Quarter horses, one of the most popular breeds in the United States. Go to the Web site if you are interested in learning about western riding, roping, reining, or barrel racing.

The Jockey Club (Thoroughbred registry)
821 Corporate Drive
Lexington, KY 40503-2794
tel: (859) 224-2700
Web site:
www.jockeyclub.com

The breed registry for Thoroughbred horses that race in the United States, Canada and Puerto Rico. Visit the Web site to learn all about racehorses in these places.

International Museum of the Horse at the Kentucky Horse Park
4089 Iron Works Parkway
Lexington, Kentucky 40511
tel: (800) 678-8813

Web site:
www.kyhorsepark.com

This museum honors man's relationship with horses and ponies. It is one of the educational highlights at the Kentucky Horse Park, where you can see and learn about many different horse and pony breeds and horse-related events.

United States Equestrian Federation (USEF)
4047 Iron Works Parkway
Lexington, KY 40511-8483
tel: (859) 258-2472
Web site: www.usef.org

Once called the Association of American Horse Shows, this organization oversees horse show rules and regulations in the United States, so that riding competitions are fair and safe for everybody.

American Riding Instructors Association (ARIA)
28801 Trenton Court
Bonita Springs, FL 34124-3337
tel: (239) 948-3232
Web site: www.riding-instructor.com
If you don't know how to find a qualified riding

instructor in your area, this Web site is a good place to start looking.

The Sugar Cubes Stables Riding School
Web site: www.sugar-cubes-ponies.com

You have met all the ponies from the Sugar Cubes Stables in this book. Now go to their Web site for information and stories about them. You can also chat with other pony lovers.

ASPCA (The American Society for the Prevention of Cruelty to Animals)
424 East 92nd Street
New York, NY 10128
tel: (800) 628-0028
Web site: www.aspca.org

The ASPCA is a charity that works to prevent cruelty to all animals. Log on to the Web site where you will find advice on your pets, stories, and lots of things to do.

Horse Illustrated
Fancy Publications
P.O. Box 6050
Mission Viejo, CA
92690-6050
Web site:
www.horseillustrated.com

Horse Illustrated is a fun magazine for all pony lovers. Look on their Web site to find out all about it and how to get your own copy. There's also useful information about breeds, horse events, and related topics.

▲ A domestic pony needs lot of care and attention.

index

This is an alphabetical list of horse and pony things that you can read about in this book. It tells you which page to go to if you want to read about grooming, rugs, or saddles, for example.

a

aids 52, 60
Alexander the Great 59
Andalusians 59
Appaloosas 11
Arab 11
asses 6
Australian ponies 55

b

Barbaro 59
bedding 32–33, 61
Bellerophon 58
bits 41, 42, 43, 60
biting 25
body language 24–25, 60
breeds 10–13, 16, 60
bridles 40, 41, 60
  fitting 43
  putting on 42–43
  taking off 42
Bucephalus 59

c

Camargues 13
canter 21, 53, 60
carrots, feeding 30, 38
Caspians 12
catching 30–31
Clydesdales 11
coat 8, 16, 28, 35, 36
colors 16–17
colts 60
conformation 14, 60
Connemara ponies 13
cowboys 11, 41

de

Dartmoor ponies 12
dismounting 51, 60

donkeys 6, 7
dressage 40,
Equidae 6
ears 8, 24
eyes 8, 23

f

Falabellas 7
families 6
famous horses 58–59
farriers 37, 61
feet 15, 36, 37
fields 35–36
Figure 59
fillies 29, 61
Fjord ponies 13
flehmen 22
foals 7, 8, 10, 28–29, 61
food 14, 21, 22, 29, 32, 38–39
freeze marks 19

g

gaits 20–21, 61
gallop 21, 54, 61
Gandalf 59
girths 40, 44, 45, 49
grass 34, 38
grazing 35, 61
grooming 36–37, 61
gymkhanas 55

h

halter 30–31, 42, 61
hands 9, 61
hay 35, 38, 39, 61
haynets 39
  filling 39
heavy horses 11, 56
herds 26–27, 61

hinnies 7
hooves 6, 15
horsepower 55
Hyracotherium 6

ijk

Icelandic horses 13
jumping 40, 55
kicking 25
Knabstrups 10

l

leading 14, 31
Lipizzaners 11
lunge line 53, 61

m

Mammoth Jacks 7
mangers 33
mares 28–29
markings 18–19
mounting 14, 48, 49, 61
mucking out 32
mules 7
mustangs 27

n

neighing 25
New Forest ponies 12
numnahs 41, 44, 45

pq

paces see gaits
Pegasus 58
points of the horse 14–15, 61
police horses 57
Przewalski's horses 6, 7, 13
quaggas 7

Quarterhorses 11
quick–release knots 31, 39

r

racehorses 11, 21, 54–55, 59
rack 21
ragwort 39
registration papers 18
reins 41, 42, 61
  holding 48, 50, 51
riding clothes 46–47
riding lessons 14, 46, 48–53
riding vacations 57
rolling 34
Roy Rogers 58
rubber matting 32, 33
rugs 34, 35, 36

s

saddles 40, 61
  putting on 44–45
  sitting in 50, 52, 53
  taking off 44
senses 22–23, 61
Shadowfax 59
shavings 32
Shetland ponies 12
Shires 11
shoes 15, 37
showing 55
skeletons 14

sleeping 9
Spanish Riding School of Vienna 11
stables 32–33
stirrups 40, 44, 49, 50
stopping 52
straw 32, 33, 61
stud books 11

t

tack 40–45, 43, 61
teeth 8, 9, 28
The Lord of the Rings 59
Thoroughbred 11
tolt 21
Trigger 58
Trojan horse 58
trot 20, 52–53, 61
turning 52
tying up 30, 31

vw

veterinarians 8, 20, 37, 61
walk 20, 52, 61
water 14, 23, 32, 35, 38
Welsh Mountain ponies 12
Welsh ponies 12, 17
western riding 41, 47, 60, 61
working horses 54–57

y

young horses 9, 27, 28, 29, 61

z

zebras 6

acknowledgments

The publisher would like to thank the following for their kind permission to reproduce their photographs:

David Waters of horsepix for all photographs except 58 bottom right and 59: Kit Houghton.

The publisher would also like to thank Port Lympne Wild Animal Park for their help with the Przewalski's horse.